Hope
From the
Dark

JoAnn Shackleford

Hope from the Dark
Copyright© JoAnn Shackleford
ISBN: 978-1-970153-14-9
Library of Congress Control Number: 2020903437

Cover Image by Shutterstock

La Maison Publishing, Inc.
Vero Beach, Florida
The Hibiscus City

Maison

Introduction

Writing is a passion for me and a gift from God. He is my inspiration for all I write. My purpose for this book is to share it with others who may walk in the dark with no hope. If it brings some light to their lives from my experience, my purpose will be fulfilled.

May each one be blessed in some way.

Walk in the light, not dark.

JoAnn Shackleford

Nancy —
a new friend to me —
I hope these Poems
bring light when you
are in a dark place —
Love,
Joann Shackleford
(2020)

Dedication

Thanks to my friend Linda Johnston for your encouragement to publish this book, for your inspiration so others may be blessed by these poems – for all the times you listen to me and pray for me – for all you did to see this book become a reality.

Your friend, JoAnn

Contents

Contemplation

I sit quietly in my chair
I'm not alone
God is there
How do I know
I hear Him in my ear
I feel His touch
So close as the air I breathe
I need Him so much
My mind wanders
My faith is there
It goes nowhere

My Jesus

My faith is strong
My body is weak
To Him, I belong
His face I seek
He gives me peace
He brings me joy
hope and love

Jump Start

Do you need a jump start
Look to your heart
Power it up
With the Holy Spirit
Get it to running
In the right way
God will help you each day

My Friend Jesus

New friends, I have made
Each time I see them
Hugs they give
Nice things they say
They inspire me and
So special I feel
I'm not more special than anyone
It's all about God's Son
He is the special one
He inspires me and
Builds me up
He fills my cup
So others can see
He lives in me
He gives me love, peace, and joy
When my Friends say nice things
It's from all to my life
Jesus brings

God

I see you there
And everywhere
The birds that sing
In the spring
The rain and snow
In the cold of winter
The leaves on the trees
As they fall to the ground
The sun so warm and
Bright in summer days
The seasons change for a reason
So, we will know and
See you in each season

Bumps in My Road

As I give God my load
My load is lighter and
Jesus shines brighter each day
He hears my prayers
Always there I am never alone
My faith is strong
Jesus faced many bumps
In His short life
All he endured was for me and you
As I strive to be like Him
There will be bumps for sure
With Him, I will endure

If I Had Wings

If I had wings, I could fly
To the sky and touch the stars
I would soar with the birds
And hear them sing
As they go from tree to tree
I could float on the clouds
So fluffy and white
If I had wings
If I could fly, I would feel so free
And not be me.
Sing with the birds and
feel the gentle breeze thru the trees
I don't have wings
I can't fly with the birds
Go from tree to tree
I can be free and be
What God created me to be
As I watch the birds fly
In the sky - So high
I am glad to be me

Youth

In our youth
We feel so free
so much to do – So much to see
We don't know the future
as we go from day to day
If we pray
God will show us His way
We race thru life all too fast
We look back
and have lost our way
We don't pray
We stumble and fall
Maybe crawl
Where is God in all of this?
At the end of the road
Waiting to help with our load.
He was there all the time
Waiting for us
To change our mind

My Journey Through Life

My journey with God
began in 1978
He gave me life and
I gave my life to Him.
It was a slow start
So much to learn.
My life took a turn
When my William became ill
And went to be with God
Was his early death God's way
To move me in His way?
I don't know – but
My faith became stronger
as I needed to trust in Him more
Kids all grown – I was all alone
Many friends were there for me
Years went by
Bible Studies – retreats
Day care kids and staff
Was so busy doing for God
Or was it for me?

Then I fell at church – broke my hip
My life was about to change forever
in ways I never imagined
Day care gone
Began rehab after surgery
God took over and Moved me to GA
to C3 – a new church – great friends
Who cared and loved me – family
God began to move in me thru the
Holy Spirit – on Sunday – the praise
team – worship service – Prayer time
For the first time in my life
I felt reborn – thru the Holy Spirit
Bible reading –Connect groups
I began to volunteer
Join the service team
In my hard times – God
made them much easier
Cancer three times – hip replacement
two blood clots – vein therapy
A pastor even prophesied over me
My writing is a gift
and blessing from my God
as I share Them with so many

I sold my house – and moved here
God said go, and I went
When we listen and follow God
He will bless us even more
I am a blessed woman
I now live and work for Him – not me
God wants good things
for all His children
After faith comes believe
Believe and keep on believing
You reap what you sow
(Joy)
(Jesus or you)

My Daughter Brenda
Dealing with Alzheimer's

Even tho I'm not me
The one you promised
to love and cherish
I still need all you can give me
I'm a mess and don't understand
how and when I changed
Even tho there are days
I don't act it - I will always love
The man who made those vows.
Why and how this came to be
Like you, I don't understand.
There are days I feel like myself, and
Other times I don't know who I am.
I know you are just as confused
With me as I am with you
No matter what I say or do
I will always need and love you.
"Mom"

Waiting

When I lie down at night
and turn out the light
The best time to pray
in the stillness of the night
I feel Him so near
As I thank Him for the day
As I fight to stay awake
I close my eyes tight
And say, Good night

God Was There

God was there all the time
To guide me all the way
So blind – I could not see
It was He leading me

So alone at the age of ten
With brothers needing me
Went from one home to another
Did not hear from our mother
Siblings separated so young
Missed my brothers
As they were with others

Years went by – I grew older
I know God was there – but where
Went to church, they talked about
Jesus God's son
I knew He was the One
Where is He?
He tried to talk to me
I couldn't hear or see

Many years later He came to me
I knew He was there
I said a prayer and
His spirit held me tight
From then on
"All with my world was right"

Stay Close to God

God is as close to us
As the air, we breathe
As the space we see
As the noise, we hear
As the touch of a hand
When we sit or stand
If we don't see, hear or feel Him
And He seems so far away
We are the one who has strayed

Your Friend

The Lord is my guiding light
To see me through the day and night.
He keeps watch over me and you.
He is our friend, kind and true
When you think you can't go it alone
And your heart has turned to stone
And you feel so alone
Just call His name – Jesus
He will run to you, pick you up
And fill your cup

Let Go, Let God

When you trust in God
and give Him your all
When you stumble
You won't fall
When you are weak
He is strong
In the midst of a dark night
He will lift you up
When you are tired
He is beside you
to carry you through
Without Him
You can do nothing
Trust Him
He's there for you

Trust

When trouble and distress
Comes your way
Do you stray or pray
God will hear what you say
He will answer
In His own way
Take time each day
to tell Him your heart
No better way
For the day to start

To Serve God

God has a Plan
For each of us
In Him to trust
It's not about us
Sometimes we let the US
get in the way to trust
We are all created by God
to serve Him and others
We have the same father
As we are sisters and brothers
His Plan is the best
He gives us peace and rest

Trust in God

Life can and does
Throw us some curves
When we least
expect them
So we try to make them
straight on our own
The curves are God's way
to help us to wait on Him
to make them straight
On God, we must wait

Praise

Our arms we raise
As to God, we praise,
For all to us, He brings
Our hands we clap
The songs we sing
All in praise for our King
Music we hear
As God's spirit is near
Praise Him,
Praise Him
As each day you pray

Nature

Nature is our gift from God
The sun to warm us and give light
The moon to shine at night
He gave His Son to light our way
The stars as they twinkle
High in the sky
Rain to help things grow
Then the beautiful rainbow
The wind and thunder
God's wake-up call for us all
Children love the snow and cold
As they skate and throw
Snowballs –it's not for all
It's all God's call
Nature changes day by day
We can change our minds and way
And thank God for each day
Whatever it brings and
See Him in everything

One Wish

If I had one wish
What would it be
Wealth, health or more stuff
When I think of all those things
True happiness they don't bring
We all want wealth
We need our health
Do we think
What does God want for us?
We go to church, we pray
We still don't know
At the end of the day.
We want so much
All God wants for us is to trust
He gives us joy and peace,
When all we have, we release
All the stuff that means so much
We can't take with us when
God we touch

The Golden Years

The years come and go
One day we are old
They call them the "Golden Years"
With them come some tears
Nothing works as it should
Days I don't feel so good
Can't see or hear
Don't remember some years
I often wonder, why am I here

The Golden Years

When I was young
Full of energy and joy
Timed moved so slow
So much I did not know
Kids grew up – moved away
Empty nesters all too soon
I could see the kids at play
Hear them say
Mom, I need you
These were the golden years
As I remembered
I shed some tears
For all the years that went so fast
I knew why I was there

New

Even today it's still
Meant for me and you
And so many still
Do not know Jesus
Or have accepted
Him as Savior
As Christians we have
a responsibility
to give Jesus to those
We know and meet
We are His hands and feet
Live our lives so bright
all can see His light

Father

You are the father of us all
We are all called
To be your witnesses
Hands and feet
Because of your love
Our hearts beat
You gave so much
When our lives you touch
Your Son on the cross
So, we won't be lost
He lives again, forgives our sin
The choice we make
The road we take
All depends on our faith

The Rain

The rain comes down
and covers the ground
The grass all wet
Rain not done yet
Clouds rolling, thunder is loud
Children running all around
The rain slows down
The sky is brighter
Clouds are lighter
Then the glow
of the beautiful rainbow

Egos

When your ego is too high
And you think you can fly
Bring yourself down
As you hit the ground!
Lift yourself up
Let Jesus fill your cup
As your ego gets smaller
Jesus gets taller

My God and Me

I said a prayer
and saw you there
Next to my chair
I heard you say
Why do you pray
I know your prayer
before you start
I'm in your heart
I'm by your side
I walk with you
I never hide
I feel your presence
all the time
Whatever I face
I feel your touch
You love me that much

Mirror View

I looked in the mirror
What did I see?
I saw me
How does God see me
How do others see me
Am I what I seem to be
The mirror is only
A reflection of who I am
God sees my heart
He knows the real me
I want to be
What God wants me to be
Mirror, mirror on the wall
Who am I

Joy

We have the joy
of Jesus each day
As we walk in His way
When to Him
Our heart we give
It is pure joy for Him to live
As you go down the street
His joy will shine
For those you meet

God Has More for You

When you think
You have arrived
And there is no more
Your faith may be strong
You are so wrong
God has much more
For you to do
Open your heart
Open the door
So God can do
A do-over in you
There is no end to what
God has for you

Food for Thought

Today...
Did you plant a seed
Help someone in need
Feed my sheep
Did you do anything for me
Did you pray
Did you hear my voice
As you go through the day
Did you make a good choice

Storms of Life

Life is a storm, full of waves
We try to be so brave
As we are tossed all around
We fuss, we cry, we ask why
Where is God
He's in the storm
And wonders
Why we can't see
Him and know
He's there for us
Don't fuss
Reach for His hand
He's there
To calm our storm
And He understands

My Day

As I rise for the day
I call your name, and I pray
When I don't know what to say
I sit and be still, and all is OK.
I know you hear
I know you are there
In my heart and everywhere
Nothing to fear – nothing to hide
When you are by my side
As you are my strength
and my guide

Blessings

Blessings are our gift from God
We have them every day
We pray and go our way
Did not see any today?
They are mostly small in our eyes
They come in any size
Expect them – Look for them
Too many to count
Each day you will be surprised
How many come
Your Way - Every day

Our Choice

We chose our way
We live each day
Sometimes life gets in the way
We don't know what to do or say
We don't even pray
when the day is good
And we go our way
We still don't pray
God is there by our side
To guide us thru
As we decide what to do
The trials we face
helps our faith to go stronger
If in God we trust
The way we chose
May not be the one
Our only way is to love
And trust God's Son
He is the only one

God Is There

I love the morning
Fresh
After a night
Of rest
The day is bright
In God's sun
Light.
What does it hold
I don't know.
Whatever is there
I am prepared
And know God is there

Life

Life is full of bumps and curves
When you begin your day
Do you stop to pray
As you go down the road
Give God your load
He's there to help
With each step
Don't go alone
Thru the day
He will guide you
Along the way

God - not Stuff

God loves us so much
Thru our lives
We gather so much stuff
Things we don't read - don't need
We hoard and still want more
Don't collect things
"Connect" with God and
Collect all the blessings
He has for you

The Christmas Tree

The Christmas tree
Standing so tall
Is like Jesus
Watching over us all
The branches remind me of Jesus
reaching out to his children
The tinsel with its glitter
Is tears Jesus must shed
When we are unkind
To one another

The garland draped
So graciously
Around the tree is like
Jesus holding you and me.
The ornaments all so different
as we are all made different

The lights shining so bright
reminds me of Jesus

The light of the world
The star at the top
Is to let us know
a Savior is born

The gifts under the tree
Is a reminder
Jesus is the greatest gift of all.
Yes, the Christmas Tree
As beautiful as it is
Will not last

But Jesus Christ
In all His Glory
IS FOREVER

PRAYER

When you are down and out
And nothing is going your way
Do you just sit and pout
Or do you kneel and pray?
If you pray everyday
Even if things go wrong
God will show you the way
With prayer, you are never alone
Talking with God is the only way
Fall on your knees and pray each day

Life

We live our lives
From day to day
Sometimes we lose our way
We walk the wrong road
And carry a heavy load
We feel lost and alone
Nowhere we belong
We turn around
And know we have found
The right way home
As the rays of the sun
Break through the dawn

The Stranger

A stranger gave me flowers today
I did not know what to say
We talked a while about her child
The flowers she gave were
Meant for his grave
As I sympathized
A tear fell from my eye
For the stranger, I met today
and promised to pray
As we parted ways
I knew in my heart
God was there that day

Stranger Who Prayed

A stranger prayed for me today
At the Dollar Tree
We talked awhile there in that isle
As she prayed for me
I prayed for her
God's spirit led her to me
At the Dollar Tree
As we walked away
She said for my items
She would pay
Thank you, I said
As the gift of receiving
Was as great as giving
A missionary from Greece
Blessed me that day
As for one another
We prayed

The Bible

The Bible is God's word
We should read it every day
Before we read
We should pray
It is our guide
With Jesus by our side
Tells us how to live
Our sins he forgives
The Bible is inspired by God
Written by men
Read it again and again

Summer

The day is sunny and bright
Children playing
In daylight
People in the park
They play till dark
Children in the pool
No one in school
The breeze is warm
The days are long
Soon summer
Will Be gone
Enjoy each day
Don't forget to Pray

The Beach

The ocean is blue
And so is the sky
The sand is warm
And so is the sun
Building sand castles
In the sand
Boy and girl walking
Hand in hand
The ocean goes forever
The sky is so high
Children running
All is happy
The sun is not so bright
The beach is quiet
All said goodnight

Faith

We have faith
In so many things
Airplanes will fly
And stay in the sky
The sun will rise
And the rain will fall
Do we hear Jesus
When He calls
Our faith is so small
Or no faith at all
Faith the size
Of a mustard seed
Is all we need
Jesus died for us
He loves us so much
Is your faith strong
Or do you have to touch

Jesus Cares

Jesus is so good to me
His love and care always there
Sometimes I don't see
All He does for me
At the end of the day
As I kneel to pray
He whispers in my ear
My love will never disappear
My eyes and ears are open wide
When I stay by His side
As He cares for me
All He wants is my loyalty
He's so good to me

The Mountain

I climbed the mountain
To see God
I went into the valley
To find God
He was not on the mountain
He was not in the valley
Is He in the air
How do I know He is there
Can I see or feel Him anywhere
I heard Him say
"My child, you can't see my face"
I don't take up space
I am "I am"
I hold you in my palm
"I am" in your heart
We will never part

NEVER TOO OLD

God created us for a reason
We are here to serve
Nothing we have we deserve
We are never too old
To serve the Lord
The joy in our heart
Gives us a good start
He knows what we can do
We just need to want to
If we need to slow down
There is always a job around
Or we can sit and do nothing
If we pray - that's something
We say we are too old
Maybe a little slow
A card we can send
Or a call we can make.
A prayer we can pray
Encourage someone along the way
You are serving God each day

Let All That You Do Be Done with Love

LOVE is more than
Silver or gold
It is there when you
Are young and old
It's always there
It will lift you up
Bring joy and
Brighten your day
When you give it away
LOVE is our gift from God
You can't love God
And not love others
We are all
Sisters and brothers
The world was created
From love
Given to us by God above

Be A Light

So much violence and
Hate in our world today
If we pray, would it go away
If we loved as He loves us
Would the hate and
violence turn to trust
The world will never be perfect
We know that can't be
For anything to change
It must start with you and me

Walk with God

The years fly by
We reach for the sky
We dream big – forget to pray
God appears one day
We have lost our way
With wide open arms
He takes our tears away
Wants to protect us from harm
Love Him – trust Him
Give Him your heart
Whatever life brings
You and Jesus will never part
He will never leave till we believe
He loves us – He is our friend
Take His hand – walk with Him
You will never be alone again

Friends

Friends are the ones
You need each day
They are always there
In joy and sorrow
You can count
On them in every way
They are here
Today and tomorrow
They never let you down
So faithful and true
Always good to have around
Real friends are so few
Say a prayer to God above
For all the friends
You have to love
Always know Jesus
Is the best friend
You will ever have

A Tribute to my Foster Parents

Forty years ago – this day
With all I owned
I came your way
I was so frightened
And all alone
You soon made me
Feel at home
You gave me love
And lots of care
And a family
I could share
If at times
I made life rough
I say thanks
For hanging tough
You were always there
You've been so great
My living with you
Was more than fate

60

God sent me there
I have no doubt
So I could learn
What love is all about
Thank you for being
Father and mother
In all this world
I would choose
No other
I love you both
So very much
Thanks to God
My life
You touched

HOMELESS

So many people without a home
Nowhere to go, they just roam
Once they had a family
They never planned their calamity

Nothing went their way
Just existed day by day
Get food wherever they can
Sleep anywhere
To get out of the rain

It's all so sad
They did nothing bad
No one should live like this
It could be us

We say we care
And what a shame
There is no one to blame
Can we change it?

What would we do if we could?
As long as homeless is not us
We say by the grace of God go I
Why should the grace of God
Apply to some and not to all?

God's grace is a gift
freely given to all His children
God loves us all
No matter the circumstances
We should not take
What we have for granted
We may someday be looking
for a place to lay our head
Be hungry or thirsty

The best way to show
God's love is helping others
Maybe what we have (material)
Gets in the way to serve God

Just maybe the homeless
have more than we do

They may truly know God
Just because of
The way they look or live
Does not mean they don't know Jesus

In Jesus' day
He would hang out
With the homeless
We have a hard time
With people
Different from us
Coming to our church

Maybe we should
Re-think
who we will welcome
To our church.
They may decide
Not to choose us

JUDGING OTHERS

Why do we find it
So easy to judge others
Someone who doesn't
Look or act like us
Jesus said
Do not judge for
You will be judged
With the same
Measure you judge others
We can't get past
The way they look
To see the real person
The person made
In the image of God
I watch "The Voice"
The coaches judge
The contestants only by
Their voices – their backs
Are turned to them
I am so glad

I am not judged
by Jesus for my appearance
He judges the heart
We are to make disciples
For him – are we
Doing that
When we face Jesus
Will he say
"I don't know you"
or "well done, my child"
Jesus said "
Feed my sheep – feed my lambs"
Are we feeding his sheep
When you go out
And invite someone to church
Give them Jesus

The Release

As I wait for the release
of the life, I now know
I wait for you, oh Lord of my soul
I am stuck in a space of the unknown
As I seek to serve the known
I need you oh Lord
In every way, every day
Your love and grace always there
As I praise you in prayer
You are my rock as the years go by
Like the morning dew
As the dawn breaks
I am born anew

The Seasons

Seasons are changing
From summer to fall
They are all in God's call
Birds singing
The earth turns green
Soon will be spring
Days are warm and long
All too soon
Summer is gone
There's a chill in the air
Leaves turn orange and brown
All are falling to the ground
Cold wind blows
Maybe some snow
Seasons are a mystery
Enjoy each one
A gift from God's Son

Tatortots

Love me now
Love me later
I will be
your sweet potato
When I am bad
don't be sad
I'll be the best
you ever had
I can be sweet
I can be mean
I can be better
than I seem
Run and hide
when you see me inside
So I can look
until you I find
If we love
one another a lot
We can have
some tatortots

Heartbeat

With every beat of my heart
I hear you calling me
So much to see – so much to be
What you created me to be
Nothing I have you need
Just my heart inside of me.
You gave it to me
I give it to you, the least I can do
With all my heart I do love you

Rainbow

The beautiful rainbow
in the sky
An awesome sight
To the eye
a gift from God
To each of us
as a promise
We can trust
The colors
so very bright
To show us
His Light
It only comes
after the rain
His promise
to proclaim

The Sun

As the sun came up
God filled my cup
Before the sun goes down
I pass it around.
So many ways to pray
Each day
For the person next door
So many more
When the sun goes down
The day is done
My cup has overrun
And once again
Gets filled

Imagine

Can you imagine
Your hand in his hand?
So much we will understand
While we are here, we trust
Until he comes for us
My hand in His
A wonderful thought
All my battles will be fought
To be so close to Him
Fills me with love
And a sense of awe
He brings me such joy
So many ways to pray each day
As we rise to exercise
When we drive down the road
Give God your load
When day is done
Pray to God's son
Take time to be still
To know God's will

God's Love

God created the universe
And each one of us
He says take care my child
It's yours for a while
Trust me in all you do
I will take care of you
I will heal
Your spirit and your soul
One day you will be made whole
I'm with you each day
You can't push me away
Dark places you will see
Come to the light
Come to me.

America

America is where I'm proud to be
A land where all can be free
To disagree and still be me
To live in peace and harmony
Freedom comes with a price
For every man and woman
Who gave their lives
And never thought twice
To do what they can
To protect our land
They make us proud
While our flag files high
With a tear in our eye
We say a prayer
"to be free"
No one should die

The Storm

The wind is blowing
There's a chill in the air
Trees begin to sway
Leaves are blowing away
Will it storm or rain?
Clouds are rolling
Thunder is not done
Lightning is bright as the sun
The day turns black
All are watching the sky
We begin to pray
For this to go away
Night comes, then the dawn
Sunrise is beautiful after the storm
Wind and rain are gone
We thank God for His care
As we come together in prayer

Reflections

As I reflect
On my journey with God
I am in awe
Of all He does
He picks me up
Puts a pen in my hand
So much I don't understand
Times I feel down
Is God still around?
Some days my pen is still
Is it His will?
He says rest my child
I have more after a while
Things happen I don't foresee
God says all in good time
It's up to me.